# What's So Great About Van Gogh?

*A Guide to Vincent Van Gogh Just For Kids*

Max Tanner

KidLit-O Books

www.kidlito.com

Cover lamge © NLshop - Fotolia.com

# Table of Contents

# About KidCaps

KidLit-O is an imprint of BookCaps™ that is just for kids! Each month BookCaps will be releasing several books in this exciting imprint. Visit are website or like us on Facebook to see more!

To add your name to our mailing list, visit this link: http://www.kidlito.com/mailing-list.html

# Introduction

Vincent van Gogh was a spectacular artist, and one that has gone down as one of the most influential artists in the history of the world. But what made this man so special? What was it about his art that made him a celebrity? During the course of his lifetime, his art was extremely unpopular—so unpopular, in fact, that van Gogh infamously cut off his own ear. His influence only became known after he had died. Why was his art not famous during his life?

He died over one hundred years ago, but we still talk about his art today. There is something peculiar about his art, something that makes it different from the works of many other artists. Vincent van Gogh was a genius, from his birth to his death, and he is an incredibly interesting person to study. He had many personal problems that both drove and destroyed his art career. Van Gogh remains one of history's most famous artists, and his art is viewed by millions of people around the world.

# Chapter 1: Early Life

Vincent van Gogh was born in the country of Holland, which is in northwestern Europe. His mother's name was Anna Cornelia Carbentus, and she was married to a reverend named Theodorus van Gogh. Theodorus was a reverend in the protestant church in Holland. Anna gave birth to her son on March 30th, 1853, in the town of Groot-Zundert. Neither of his parents knew that, one day, their son would grow up to be one the most hated, and the most loved, artists of all time.

Vincent grew up with three sisters and two brothers: Elisabeth, Wil, Anna, Theo, and Cor. While not much is known about Vincent van Gogh's childhood, we do know that he did not spend much time drawing or practicing to be an artist. However, Vincent's mother, Anna Cornelia Carbentus, enjoyed painting. It is thought that her love of art was passed down to her son, even if Vincent didn't like art right away. Anna liked painting watercolors, something that Vincent would experiment with down the road.

*Watercolor painting* involves paint that is partly made of water, giving the colors a clear and bright look. It is this bright look that defined many of Vincent van Gogh's most famous paintings. When studying van Gogh, it is crucial to understand why he started painting watercolors, or where he learned all of his information. We can assume that his mother played a strong role in his education as an artist!

As Vincent grew up, his parents noticed that he was a moody child. Vincent was often sad and angry, but no one knew entirely why at the time. He stayed in school until he was fifteen years old. When he was fifteen, his parents barely had enough money to keep the family going. It was difficult to feed six children and two parents. Vincent needed to quit school in order to find a job, something he did not really want to do. Even though he left school early, though, Vincent was still able to speak Dutch, English, German, and French fluently.

At first he was not sure where he wanted to get a job. Eventually, he worked with his Uncle Cornelis, who sold art for a living. His Uncle Cornelis worked with the Hague, which was a center for art in Holland. He worked there for six years until he was sent to London to work at a place called the Groupil Gallery.

Vincent had always wanted to visit London, and when he was there he became enamored with the city. He loved the city, he loved the people, and he loved British writers. He was a big fan of Charles Dickens, the author of famous classics like *Great Expectations*, *A Tale of Two Cities*, *Oliver Twist*, and the popular children's story, *A Christmas Carol*. While he was in England, he also enjoyed visiting many of the art galleries that the country had to offer. It is likely that he began to like art more and more, thinking about it more often. English art had a profound influence on van Gogh's life.

While in London, he also fell in love. There was a woman named Eugenie Loyer who caught his eye immediately, and Vincent was infatuated with her. He loved her so much, in fact, that he asked for her hand in marriage. Unfortunately, however, Eugenie said no.

Vincent could not handle the rejection; it nearly destroyed him. He had an emotional breakdown, and was not exactly sure what to do with his life. His love for her had been everything, and it was suddenly thrown away. He got rid of all of his books, except for one: the Bible. Vincent was raised in a religious household, especially since his father was a reverend for the protestant church. Vincent decided that he was going to spend his life serving God instead, ignoring his career in the world of art.

At the Groupil Gallery, the managers soon became acutely infuriated with Vincent, who was telling his customers not to waste their money on art, since he believed that art was not majorly important. The Groupil Gallery started losing business, and no one wanted to interact with the sad, angry van Gogh. The managers fired him, and Vincent van Gogh no longer had a job.

At this point, he was unsure of where to go, or what he wanted to do with religion. He decided to teach and preach the word of God, in a Methodist school and in a church. Vincent surrounded himself with many religious preachers and decided that he would like to become a minister, like his father. He was told that, in order to become a minister, he would need to go to Amsterdam, where the School of Theology was. *Theology* is the study of religion. The part *"theo"* means "god," and the part *"ology"* means "the study of." Put them together, and you get "the study of god."

But there was one thing that stopped Vincent from getting into the school. He studied hard for a whole year because each student needed to take multiple tests before getting into the school. One of these exams was on the Latin language—a language that Vincent was known for hating. He thought that cultured people around the world should no longer speak Latin and that only poor people should speak it. When the school discovered this, they were offended refused to allow Vincent in.

Dismayed yet again, Vincent decided to go the Church of Belgium. By this point, he was twenty-five years old and desperate to find solid work. He went into the coal mines of southern Belgium, a filthy, nasty place where workers never wanted to go. Vincent's job was to preach the word of God to the miners, and also to take care of them when they were sick. It was not the best job in the world, but Vincent did enjoy what he was doing. He enjoyed leading the miners' faith.

In the mines, he even began drawing pictures of the workers. The miners loved seeing their drawings, and Vincent was happy to draw them. He did not stay there for too long though. After two years, the committee that ran the Church of Belgium decided that they did not like the following that Vincent was getting in the mines. Too many people liked him, and they liked him so much that they even compared him and his preaching with that of Jesus Christ. Because of this, he was fired from the Church of Belgium.

Three times already, Vincent van Gogh felt like his life had been smashed to pieces. He felt like a failure at love, at education, and at preaching. What was left for him? He thought he might try to return to the art business—but this time, he would not be selling art. He would be creating it.

Vincent contacted his younger brother Theo, who was an art dealer like their uncle. Theo told Vincent that he would be able to give him enough money to support him for a while, until he found success as an artist. Vincent moved to Brussels, the capital of Belgium.

There was just one slight problem. Vincent van Gogh had no professional education whatsoever. Unlike many of history's other notable artists, he did not have daily practice. He did not show promise when he was a young child. He had never been an apprentice, he had never gone to art school, and people did not know him for his art. As a man in his twenties, he would have to start all over again.

Vincent began to teach himself art, reading many books on the subject and practicing on his own. He hoped that if he devoted himself wholly, he would find success. Eventually, his art became better and better, and he found that art made him happy. Despite this happiness, however, Vincent's love life caused trouble for him.

After his horrible rejection from Eugenie, Vincent fell in love with his cousin. At the time, it was not unusual for cousins to marry each other. Today, we think of that as wrong, but back then it happened quite often. His cousin rejected him, however, and Vincent was left alone once again. He fell in love with another woman named Clasina Maria Hoornik, who was not the greatest influence on Vincent.

Vincent van Gogh's family despised Clasina, and they told Vincent that they would stop sending him money unless he broke up with her. Reluctantly, Vincent agreed. His family's money was the only thing keeping him alive. If it were not for his brother Theo, Vincent's art career would never have started.

Angry, sad, and confused, Vincent fled Belgium to live in the Netherlands. He did not have a single home, but instead he moved around from place to place. During his time there, he painted the people, and he painted the beautiful landscapes. This was part of his practicing, something that would help his art later on.

# Chapter 2: Van Gogh's Health Problems

Van Gogh is known for his popular art, but he is also known for many of the health issues that he suffered from. He had many *mental disabilities*, problems that involved his mind. Today, when some people think of an "artist," they think of someone who is moody and sad, usually thinking about life and all of the bad things in it. It is because of van Gogh that this image exists. He was the original brooding artist.

The first disability that van Gogh suffered from was something called *bipolar disorder*, which involves a person's emotions. *Bipolar disorder* makes someone feel tremendously excited and then majorly depressed, with no reason or justifiable change. Van Gogh would often paint remarkably quickly, without stopping, and then he would feel sad for several days. He would feel depressed, as if no one in the world loved him. His rejection from schools and tough love life only made his bipolar disorder worse.

Van Gogh was also an avid writer—too avid, though. He enjoyed writing so much that many doctors believed he had *hypergraphia*, which is when a person will continue to write without stopping. We have evidence of van Gogh's obsessive writing, and many websites have transcriptions of the hundreds of letters he wrote during the course of his life.

Van Gogh was prone to seizures, which means he got them a lot. A *seizure* is when someone with a certain condition loses control of their body, falling onto the ground, their muscles causing them to flail around. It is believed that the medicine he took for his seizures may also have caused him to see the color yellow everywhere. What is odd about this is that the color yellow is featured in a number of van Gogh paintings.

He also suffered from a couple conditions of poisoning. The first type is called *thujone poisoning,* which he got from drinking too much alcohol. Van Gogh thought that alcoholic beverages might help with his seizures and his depression, but he was wrong—it only made things worse. The chemical *thujone* also causes people to see objects in the color yellow, possibly another reason van Gogh loved the color.

*Lead poisoning* was the other type. He got this from using paint that had lead in it, and chewing pieces of dried paint. On many occasions, when van Gogh was feeling depressed, he even tried to drink the paint, because he thought it would kill him. Van Gogh's *bipolar disorder* made it extremely hard to live, and he often thought that death might be better. Luckily, he stayed alive for quite a while.

Van Gogh did much of his painting out in the sun. He wanted all of his paintings to feel real, so he would paint outside. In fact, van Gogh spent so much time outside that he often had *sunstroke*, which is when the heat would make his stomach feel bad. He felt nauseous and moody, and often got angry towards people.

Van Gogh's mental disabilities were a gargantuan problem in his life, and to cope with them took a lot of effort and willpower. Often they interrupted his painting and made him feel horrible about his work. His painting, however, sometimes acted as a cure for all of his problems.

# Chapter 3: Becoming an Artist

Vincent van Gogh lived at a time when there many changes going on in the world. People were exploring art in new ways. During the 1800s, there was a popular artistic movement called *impressionism*. This was a technique that artists used to create paintings. By using lots of bright colors, the artists believed they that were giving a new feeling to their work. *Impressionist* artists needed to use bright colors, but also to paint the world around them very realistically.

Van Gogh, however, was not strictly an impressionist. He was part of a movement called *post-impressionism.* An artist who identified as *post-impressionist* wanted to do more than just paint the world around them. They wanted the paintings to convey feelings and emotion, and they wanted to experiment with the bright colors that they used. *Post-impressionism* is just like *impressionism,* except that there are not as many rules. Van Gogh liked having freedom in what he painted.

The art that van Gogh made helped him cope with his mental disabilities. After being rejected from preaching and his romantic life, art was the only thing he had. Many different people and things influenced his life as an artist.

For one, he was inspired by the impressionist movement. If he had never seen impressionist art, he would never have become a post-impressionist. He looked at art by famous artists like Henri de Toulouse-Lautrec and Pisarro, both popular among art-lovers at the time, and even art-lovers today.

To enhance his education, van Gogh even enjoyed looking at the works of Japanese artists. He found eastern culture to be magnificently interesting. He had always wanted to go to Japan, but his dream was never realized.

In the year 1888, when Vincent van Gogh was thirty-five years, he moved in the countryside in southern France. Despite the fact that his brother Theo was supporting him financially, he still received remarkably little money and was having trouble surviving. Paint, after all, was expensive. How was he supposed to stay healthy and still have enough money for paint?

This is when he began eating paint. He ate little else besides coffee and bread, and he began suffering physically as well as mentally. Yet he still continued to paint, even if he was in a supremely unhealthy state.

Theo was extremely worried about his brother Vincent's health. When he heard that Vincent was not looking too good, he called upon the artist Paul Gauguin. Paul was also a post-impressionist artist, who was good friends with Vincent van Gogh and his family. Theo asked Gauguin if he could check on Vincent and make sure that everything is okay.

Gauguin arrived at Vincent van Gogh's tiny yellow house hidden in the French countryside, and he stayed there for a while. However, his stay with Vincent was not happy. Vincent van Gogh was moody and often liked to argue and fight with Gauguin. One night, their arguments got particularly heated, and Gauguin stormed out of the house. Van Gogh followed him, and Gauguin saw that he had a razor in his hand. But van Gogh then disappeared.

That night, van Gogh cut off his own ear. This was a result of the emotional problems that he was suffering from, and his intense fights with Gauguin. Van Gogh felt like no one appreciated his art, and his lack of money upset him deeply. He hated not having food on the table to feed himself; he hated being in his thirties and not having a wife or children; he hated no one buying his art; and he hated that his brother had to send someone to keep an eye on him. On top of that, Vincent van Gogh's fluctuating moods did not help him at all.

So, drastically and unnecessarily, he took his own ear. The next morning, French police took him to a hospital called Hotel-Dieu hospital. Van Gogh ended up okay, but he did suffer from the loss of a lot of blood. The blood loss made him weak, and made him have even more seizures than normal. The doctors took care of Van Gogh for a few weeks, until he was finally released in the first week of 1889.

Like most of his life, Vincent van Gogh emerged from the hospital feeling alone and depressed, despite the moral and financial support of his brother Theo. Van Gogh thought that he would be able to find peace and happiness in painting, so he decided to return to art and the yellow house in which he lived. Until that happiness came, however, he knew that he would need to keep checking in at the hospital.

Vincent van Gogh lived in his home by day, and at night he would visit the hospital so that he could check in with the doctors. None of this helped, though. The people of the town had heard that van Gogh was a dangerous man. They wanted nothing to do with him. They wanted him gone, and gone for good.

The people were so angry that they all signed a petition, declaring that van Gogh should be moved to an *asylum*, a place where people with mental disabilities can receive help on a daily basis. When van Gogh heard about this, he was so ashamed that he decided to listen to the petition, and he admitted himself into the Saint-Paul-de-Mausole mental asylum.

Even in the asylum, however, he continued working on his art. Many of the paintings that he created in the asylum were shown to the public on art displays. This included "Starry Night," one of Vincent van Gogh's most famous works. Because of his bipolar disorder, he went on a painting frenzy, sometimes finishing one painting per day. This was an incredible feat, and yet van Gogh was never truly happy.

Despite the fact that his art was good, it was not as popular as he thought it should have been. He was constantly unhappy with his work, only believing that people everywhere hated it and hated him.

# Chapter 4: The Potato Eaters

Today, people would pay millions of dollars for an original copy of one of Vincent van Gogh's paintings. It may be hard to believe, but he only sold a single painting during the course of his life. It sold for four hundred francs in 1890, which roughly equals seventy-eight dollars in today's American currency. His paintings did not become well known until after his death, which we will talk about later.

Many of Vincent van Gogh's works, even if people did not realize it at the time, were incredible, deep, and meaningful.

*The Potato Eaters* was one of van Gogh's first paintings and, posthumously, one of his most popular. *Posthumously* means after someone's death. Van Gogh finished painting The Potato Eaters in 1885, when he was still learning exactly how to paint. If you look at this painting and many of his later works, you can see that his skill really improved over time. But still, The Potato Eaters is a hugely impressive painting!

If you have not seen the painting, it shows five people eating potatoes around a dinner table. The painting is quite dark, which contrasts with many of van Gogh's later, brighter works. It is likely that he had not totally committed to post-impressionism yet.

What was van Gogh trying to do when he painted The Potato Eaters? Well, his artistic goal was to create a realistic work. He wanted his audience to feel like they were sitting at the table with the people in the picture, to hear their conversation, to see their illuminated faces. But when you look at the painting, it may be easy to overlook all of the details in the background. Vincent van Gogh paid special attention to the background, making sure that every inch of the painting was given equal focus. He believed that this would give it a realistic look, and he indeed achieved his goal.

What about the subject of the painting? What does it mean? It is clear to see that the five people in the painting are poor; they are most likely peasants, a common term for lower-class citizens in the 1800s and beyond. It is important to note that *potatoes* are commonly a sign for poverty. Since they grow in plenty and are harvested by many poor farmers, many peasants ate them. Besides the potatoes, though, the room in the painting is dark and the wood looks battered and slightly rotted.

No one in the painting has a happy expression on his or her face, and they look thin and bony. Their clothes are ragged and dirty; generally, they look like friends or family that has been working hard all day, and has come together at night to share food. Although there is no truly clear answer, Vincent van Gogh seems to be discussing the tough lives of the poor—something he would know very well since he struggled for money most of his life. It is possible that the somber and disappointed faces of the people in the painting also reflect many of his emotions.

Not only the people show sadness in the painting, though. The colors themselves are an indication of the painting's message. Most of the colors are dark, which sets the *tone*, or the feel, of the work. The only bright colors can be seen on the faces of the people, mixed in with shadows, showing their sharp and brooding features. Many of the colors in the painting are brown, gray, and green, colors that are associated with dirt and the earth, and also farming. This can represent all of the work that the peasants have been doing all day.

Many art scholars have called the painting *naturalist*, meaning that van Gogh painted things exactly as they should be painted. He did exaggerate anything within the painting, and all of the colors appear precisely as they normally would look inside the potato eaters' house. No light in the painting appears out of thin air; van Gogh does an excellent job with shading and recognizing that, in a house of peasants, the residents might not be able to afford the best light source.

So, now that you know what The Potato Eaters is all about, it's important to think about why it is important. Why should you care about this at all? This painting is a perfect example of how an author might reflect his or her feelings in her work—but not blatantly. This painting has a lot of meaning once you know more about Vincent van Gogh's life. When you think that he was poor, had barely any food, and was suffering from extreme sadness, you might feel some of this too, and even get a better understanding of what van Gogh went through.

Also, this painting most likely resonated with many of the peasants at the time, even if it did not become immediately popular. Not only does The Potato Eaters represent van Gogh's physical and mental state, it also gives a face to the troubles of many poor people at the time. This painting is a window into history, and a window into one of history's greatest and most intriguing minds.

# Chapter 5: Vincent van Gogh and the Sunflowers

During the course of his lackluster artist career, Vincent van Gogh also experimented with a type of art called *still life*. Still life art is when the artist looks at an inanimate object and paints it just as it is, as someone walking by might see it. This was part of the *naturalist* movement, to paint things in their natural environment. Some of van Gogh's favorite things to paint were sunflowers. There are plenty examples of this.

The sunflower paintings demonstrate van Gogh's obsession with color yellow, as yellow is something that is often associated with sunflowers. Many of the paints have bright colors, but the sunflower paints can also show us something else about van Gogh, and something else about the nature of his art.

When we think of flowers, we usually think of life. We may even think of love. But what we do not usually think about is that flowers will always wilt and die eventually because they are living organisms. There are plenty of van Gogh paintings that show bright, lively flowers; but there are also plenty of van Gogh paintings that show dying flowers, using darker shades of yellow, and also colors such as dark orange, brown, and gray.

Looking at one single sunflower painting might not be that impressive, but when you look at all of them side-by-side, you can begin to see the contrasts and the comparisons between them. This bigger picture idea also relates to Vincent van Gogh and the mental problems he was enduring at the time. His moods switched from extremely excited and happy (*bright colors*) to sad and melancholy (*dark colors*). This is another reason that the sunflower paints are so extraordinary, despite the fact that they look so plain and simple at first.

So, what else makes them noteworthy? Why should students be paying attention to Vincent van Gogh's paintings of flowers? After his death, when people began to see the true beauty of his art, they realized what kinds of messages he was sending. Van Gogh's paintings were so simple, but they were able to convey such extreme emotions, felt by all humans and everyone who looks at them. Many people have tried to capture the emotion of van Gogh's paintings, but no one seems to succeed. Perhaps, because van Gogh felt so emotionally tied to his work, he was able to better put his feelings into his art.

The sunflowers are one good example of his still life, but Vincent van Gogh of course used other flowers in his work. He also enjoyed using irises and roses, some of his favorite flowers. Most of the time, he was unable to afford human models that he could paint, so finding flowers in the woods was an easy—and inexpensive—task. One of his best-known works, titled Irises, came from this.

He began work on Irises while in the mental asylum, after seeing irises there. Irises does not feature the swirly, warm style that is seen in many of Vincent van Gogh's paintings. It instead takes a rough, though realistic, approach, to a very beautiful scene—most likely something that not many art scholars had seen at the time, but that did not immediately come off as impressive.

Irises can currently be viewed in Los Angeles, California, at the Getty Center. It is one the most expensive paintings in the world! It was sold for fifty-four million dollars in the late eighties and might be even more expensive now.

# Chapter 6: On A Dark and Starry Night

Before starting the painting *Starry Night,* Vincent van Gogh wrote that "At present I absolutely want to paint a starry sky. It often seems to me that night is still more richly coloured than the day; having hues of the most intense violets, blues and greens. If only you pay attention to it you will see that certain stars are lemon-yellow, others pink or a green, blue and forget-me-not brilliance. And without my expatiating on this theme it is obvious that putting little white dots on the blue-black is not enough to paint a starry sky."

Before diving into the subject of the painting, this quotation demonstrates that van Gogh is willing to see beyond the fact that night is dark. He sees the dark colors as beautiful, and the bright colors of the stars as something to marvel and wonder at.

*Starry Night* is most likely Vincent van Gogh's most popular painting, and arguably one of the most famous paintings in the history of the world. Not many paintings have been replicated and reproduced as many times as Starry Night has. Why is this? What makes Starry Night so captivating and special? It did not follow van Gogh's typical post-impressionist style, instead depicting the world as swirling and perhaps slightly disproportionate.

The painting Starry Night is mainly taken up by the swirling sky, which has different shades of blue and white. The moon and seven stars rest in the sky, casting light on the blue sky around them. The sky seems to have been painted with thick brush strokes that give the sky a sort of movement, almost like the waves of an ocean, a key to note for later. Below the sky sits a town with many houses and what appears to be a church steeple towering above everything else.

But many people notice the large, curvy, shadowy object that takes up a good portion of the painting on the left side—and no one is exactly sure what it is. Some people think it is a mountain, others think it is a castle, and some people think it is a bush or some form of vegetation.

The colors in Starry Night are contrasting, yet they go really well together. In the small town, many of the houses are dark. The darkness would usually bring up images of sadness and hate, but the audience does not get this image since some of the windows are illuminated. The town looks quiet and cozy and peaceful, something that van Gogh may have always wanted, but never actually achieved.

Once again, in Starry Night, you can see that van Gogh uses the color yellow. The color yellow is notable because it is the only vivid color in the dark sky. In fact, the color yellow is why the painting is called "Starry Night" in the first place; the stars need to have some importance!

It is clear that "light" is a truly crucial part of the painting. So what does "light" mean? Why should you focus on the "light" in Starry Night? Light is typically seen as something helpful. If you are walking on a dark path, the light from the moon and the stars can help you on your way. Van Gogh may have felt this way about a lot of things in life. While The Potato Eaters is a pessimistic—or a *negative*—painting, Starry Night appears hopeful. The colors are warm and beautiful, and you can feel hope when you look at it.

Many people think that the sky is another way of looking at the human mind—especially Vincent van Gogh's mind. Much of the time, he was confused. The swirling sky represents van Gogh's swirling and confused thoughts—and the light is the light at the end of the tunnel, the happiness that he can reach.

Scholars and professors who study art have noted that there are two main aspects of the painting: there is nature, and there are humans. While we do not physically see any humans, we know that they are there because there are houses and a church. While normally nature and humans are seen as two different things, everything in the painting seems to blend together and act as one. The painting is very even and harmonious, and easy to look at and grasp.

Despite the fact that humans and nature are living together, the humans appear to be asleep since there is no motion in the town; everything is still. The sky and the hills, however, were painted were curving brushstrokes. Van Gogh made it look like everything was in motion, like an ocean wave.

Starry Night may not be the most realistic painting; it is certainly not as realistic as The Potato Eaters. The sky and hills are not accurately painted, some of the colors are disjointed, and so on. So, strictly, Starry Night is not an *impressionist* painting, which wants to paint things truthfully and realistically. However, it is a *post-impressionist* painting because it focuses more on van Gogh's emotions and breaking the traditional rules of impressionism.

# Chapter 7: A Self-Portrait of the Artist as a Young Man

During a three-year period, Vincent van Gogh created thirty self-portraits, all of them just a few years before he died. Many artists complete self-portraits, but what makes them so special? Why should we care what Vincent van Gogh's self-portraits look like? Well, when we examine what they truly mean to the artist, we get a deeper insight into their minds.

Artists are praised for their creative minds. So what happens when a creative mind thinks about itself? Van Gogh, as the original brooding artist, was a man of *introspection*, which means that he often thought about himself, his character, and his purpose in life. He used painting as a way to look upon himself, and to paint more than just his physical appearance. He thought that certain things within the painting could tell people what he was really like.

He only started doing self-portraits because he did not have enough money to pay for models to paint. So, who else better to paint than himself? It would save him money, plus he could probably learn a lot about himself. There are plenty of places where you find a full collection of Vincent van Gogh's self-portraits on the Internet, and you can measure the changes across the years, perhaps aligning his portraits with his life events.

It is fascinating to see the portraits of van Gogh before and after he severed his ear. While the self-portraits before the event make him look very realistic and proper, the one in which he has a bandage covering the right side of his face also makes his face look distorted, pale, and lifeless—perhaps representing how he felt at the time his depression was taking its toll on him.

# Chapter 8: Van Gogh's Letters

Vincent van Gogh left more than just artwork behind. He is especially known for the letters that he left behind. Hundreds of them were recorded. Online, students can find the mostly complete correspondence that occurred between Vincent and his brother Theo.

It is one thing to study Vincent van Gogh's life, and it is quite another to read the loving words exchanged between him and his brother. It adds a new level of personality to Vincent and his distraught character. If you search for the letters on the Internet, you can see what Theo and Vincent were talking about—and there are literally hundreds of them, approximately nine hundred to be exact.

The letters are a good way to get inside the mind of van Gogh. What was he feeling at this point in his life? How was he communicating with Theo? Since Theo was the only reason that van Gogh was able to survive, giving him money and shelter when needed, the relationship between van Gogh and Theo is extremely important.

It's not just that there are so *many* letters that survived the test of time, but the fact that the letters themselves reveal so much about van Gogh's life. Hundreds of artists have left behind their letters to loved ones, but none of them tell historians so much as the ones of Vincent van Gogh do. Just by reading the letters, one can journey with the artist as he searches for his true calling as a child, grows up with many issues, and struggles to find comfort and support in his time as an artist.

There is an excellent example of the quality of van Gogh's letters. In one of them, he writes:

> "What am I in the eyes of most people — a nonentity, an eccentric, or an unpleasant person — somebody who has no position in society and will never have; in short, the lowest of the low. All right, then — even if that were absolutely true, then I should one day like to show by my work what such an eccentric, such a nobody, has in his heart. That is my ambition, based less on resentment than on love in spite of everything, based more on a feeling of serenity than on passion. Though I am often in the depths of misery, there is still calmness, pure harmony and music inside me. I see paintings or drawings in the poorest cottages, in the dirtiest corners. And my mind is driven towards these things with an irresistible momentum."

This quotation shows us a lot about van Gogh. He says that he is distraught and sad a lot of the time—but despite these rough feelings, he still manages to push through, find the happy things in life, and put them into his paintings. This would explain why, even though he suffered from so many dark thoughts, the subject of his art is bright. He still finds that he wants to show "love."

# Chapter 9: How to Van Gogh Around the World

There is one thing that is incredibly important to understand about the life of Vincent van Gogh: the places he lived influenced his painting. *Location* played a huge part in his life, especially because he spent so much time moving from place to place and not having a real home. Many people say that this is also one of the reasons that he was so troubled all of the time. Whatever the reasons, though, van Gogh was a traveler, and if we want to understand his life, we have to understand where he had been.

Many people who visit Europe go on "Van Gogh Tours," in which they explore all of the places that Vincent van Gogh lived, in order to get a better idea of his life. If you wish to do this, it is a lot of fun (although it can get expensive), although this section will explore the importance of many of the settings in Vincent's life.

*Vincent's Hometown*

Unfortunately, the house where Vincent van Gogh was born is no longer standing. It was destroyed in 1903 and rebuilt. The new building, however, is the site of the Vincent van GoghHuis. This is a museum of all things van Gogh, and a great place for people to visit if they wish to learn more about the artist's childhood and general history.

*Arles, France*

In the city of Arles, France, there are many intriguing places about the life of artist Vincent van Gogh. If you ever visit the city, the Arles Visitor Center will have plenty of information of van Gogh's life and the cool places you can go. In Arles, you can visit places that were the inspiration for many of van Gogh's paintings, such as Starry Night Over the Rhone. It is extremely intriguing to see the scenery that van Gogh once saw so that we can understand his world better!

The Café van Gogh sits in Arles, France and remains a popular tourist attraction today. The building was not always called the Café van Gogh, however. Vincent used to paint here, and this building is the subject of his work, Café Terrace at night. If you look at pictures of the café now, and pictures of Vincent's famous painting, you can see the similarities immediately. Vincent painted this work on that spot, and so it is a popular area for tourists and art historians to flock to.

Many teachers, when telling their students about Vincent van Gogh, like to simulate a café in class, as a fun experiment in the type of food that Vincent might have been eating at the time (and it is delicious too!). In addition to this, many cafes that are van Gogh-themed have sprung up across the United States and some countries in Europe. Van Gogh has become a cultural icon in many places.

If you ever get the chance to visit Arles, France, you may also want to stop by the L'Espace Van Gogh, which is the new name of the hospital at which Vincent van Gogh cut off his own ear. Vincent even painted certain areas of the hospital's courtyard outside, so visitors are able to see exactly where van Gogh stood and painted, and what he saw through his own eyes.

Also in Arles, France is the Langlois Bridge, which was a popular place frequented by van Gogh. During the course of his life, van Gogh became obsessed with Japanese architecture and art. The western name for this at the time was *Japonisme*. When van Gogh was living, the world was not as *integrated* as it is today—there was not a lot of trade between different countries, like you see every day now. In 1856, Japan opened trade with many western European nations, so van Gogh saw an increase in Japanese artifacts.

Japonisme might be one of the reasons that van Gogh's later paintings were so bright. Much of Japanese art contained many bright and pure colors. Japanese art also involved depictions with strong outlines, one of the reasons that van Gogh's art was so popular and revolutionary. He also liked to have many contrasting colors in his paintings, very similar to the characteristics of Japanese artwork. Van Gogh painted a lovely picture of the Langlois Bridge, and you can compare his painting with the real thing!

In the town of *Auvers-sur-Oise*, there are a couple places that held extreme significance in the life of Vincent van Gogh. He painted an image of the garden of his doctor, Dr. Gachet, but the painting was created with a decidedly odd style. The brush strokes are more wavy and squiggly than usual, and many of the colors of darker, which could have represented van Gogh's state of mind while he painted the garden.

In addition to that, tourists can also visit *Le Maison de van Gogh. Maison* in French means "house." *Le Maison de van Gogh* actually used to be the inn of the Ravoux family, who helped him in his final days. Today, vistors are able to tour the inside and see the room where van Gogh died. The inn is still an operating restaurant, and it serves many of the traditional meals that van Gogh ate during his time there.

Finally, you can visit the grave of Vincent van Gogh. It sits at the top of a hill. Van Gogh was buried next to his brother, Theo. The two graves sit among a garden of vivid green plants with purple flowers sparkling throughout them. These plants and flowers were planted by the son of Dr. Gachet, in loving memory of the van Gogh brothers.

*The Van Gogh Museum*

In Amsterdam sits the Van Gogh Museum, where tourists will find dozens of paintings and artifacts from the life of Vincent van Gogh. The painting *The Potato Eaters* rests in this museum, along with plenty of sunflower paintings. The items on exhibit are divided into different times that they were painted in van Gogh's life, so that visitors are able to see how his paintings might have changed over time, and with his changing thoughts.

Most of these artifacts and paintings had belonged to Theodore van Gogh after Vincent died, but they have since been put into the museum so that the world can have access to van Gogh's mind and his life. In addition to paintings from van Gogh, other works stand in the museum, many of them piece of art created by impressionist and post-impressionist artists.

It is sad that all of this great art can only be held in a single place, but it is an exciting visit for anyone who can make the journey. The museum puts Vincent's landscape paintings, self-portraits, portraits, drawings, still lives, and other assorted works up for audiences to view and consider. The museum draws in hundreds of thousands of people each year, all wanting to get a better idea of van Gogh's life and his artwork.

# Chapter 10: The Death of Van Gogh

While Vincent van Gogh was in the asylum, his first and only painting sold during his life. His painting, "The Red Vineyards" had been in the possession of his brother Theo, and it had sold for four hundred trancs, the French form of money. Despite this victory in a sea of troubling debt and hopelessness, van Gogh's mental problems persisted. Theo desperately tried to find a doctor who tackle the problems that Vincent faced.

A man by the name of Dr. Paul Gachet was found, and he agreed to help Vincent. Van Gogh moved closer to Dr. Gachet, even though nothing good came of it. Instead of being helpful, the doctor and Vincent's family criticized him for the way in which he was spending, which destroyed Vincent. He thought that his family no longer supported his art career and that Theo would stop trying to get people to buy his art.

At this point in his life, he lived at an inn. He would often paint portraits of the innkeeper's thirteen year-old daughter, whose name was Adeline Ravoux. She spent much time with Vincent van Gogh, calling him "Monsieur Vincent" and enjoying his company. Adeline never saw that something might have been troubling van Gogh.

Theo knew that something was wrong with Vincent once again, and encouraged him to see Dr. Gachet. Vincent, however, refused to admit that anything was wrong. He said that all of his troubles and worries were far away. Even though Theo saw that Vincent was troubled in his letters, the innkeeper and his family saw nothing wrong. Each day, Vincent woke up at the same time, ate breakfast, and painted the morning away. He would eat lunch and dinner at the same time and he always spent the afternoon writing letters or spending time with the innkeeper's family. Nothing seemed out of the ordinary.

One morning, though, everything changed.

Vincent woke up normally, at the same time as always, and ate breakfast at the inn. He left to go paint. . . but he never came back for lunch. And he never came back for dinner. The innkeeper and his family began to worry. Why did Vincent not come back? He had had the same schedule for weeks, never breaking it.

At nine o'clock that night, Vincent returned to the inn. He was walking strangely—he was bent over and clutching his stomach. The innkeeper's husband said to Vincent, "Monsieur Vincent, we were anxious, we are happy to see you to return; have you had a problem?"

Vincent van Gogh only replied, "No, but I have. . ."

He never finished his sentence, so we will never know what he truly wanted to say. Some historians have tried to complete his sentence, but there is no way to know for sure. The Ravoux family knew that something was terribly wrong. After Vincent climbed upstairs and staggered into his room, the innkeeper went to his door to see if he could hear anything.

The innkeeper heard some moaning from the room, and decided to go in. What he saw shocked him. Vincent van Gogh lay on the bed, his hand closed on his chest. The innkeeper asked what was wrong, and Vincent lifted his hand and his shirt. There was a bullet hole in his chest. The innkeeper was horrified and asked what had happened.

Distraught, Vincent van Gogh had taken a pistol that morning, determined to finally kill himself. In July, He took a bullet to the chest—but as he failed in his art, so too did he fail in suicide. He bled profusely and fell unconscious, which is why he did not return for lunch and for dinner. At night, he woke up and realized that he was not dead but that he had survived his bullet. He returned to the inn, where he came across the innkeeper and his family.

When the innkeeper heard this story, he immediately called for Dr. Gachet, who came immediately. Dr. Gachet treated Vincent van Gogh's wounds, fearing that, even though van Gogh hadn't died yet, he would not have too much time left.

In the hospital, Vincent realized that maybe he did not want to die. He was indeed surrounded by family that was loving and willing to take care of him—perhaps he was wrong to try to take his own life. In one of his letters, he noted that "Close friends are truly life's treasures. Sometimes they know us better than we know ourselves. With gentle honesty, they are there to guide and support us, to share our laughter and our tears. Their presence reminds us that we are never really alone." This shows that van Gogh did truly care about the family and friends that surrounded him and that, despite all of his sadness and his anger, he knew that people did, in fact, care about him.

That night, as he lay in bed, he knew that he did not have much time left. Vincent turned to his brother Theo and asked to be taken home. Vincent van Gogh just wanted to go home. Unfortunately, however, this never happened.

A day after he shot himself, Vincent van Gogh died from loss of blood. He died at 1:30 in the morning.

Other people, however, say that there is a different story about van Gogh's death.

This story sets Vincent leaving the innkeeper's house at the normal time, like he did everyday. In the fields, as he was doing his early morning painting, he encountered two brothers, who were known to have been particularly mean to Vincent. One of the brothers was only sixteen years-old, but still they would play pranks on him and insult him and make him feel horrible about his art.

This story says that the two brothers tainted van Gogh's coffee with salt (which would give it an awful taste) and hid snakes in his paint box for him to find. Van Gogh was furious at the two boys, but he refused to punish them. One of the boys had a pistol with him, and he accidentally fired. The bullet shot off and went into van Gogh's chest.

Van Gogh, though, wanted to die, so he claimed that it was a suicide attempt so that the boys would not get in any trouble.

Which story do you believe? The first story is the one that most historians and scholars find the most credible, since the second story is mostly guesswork, and the facts do not seem to fully support it.

Vincent van Gogh's funeral was incredibly sad. All of his family and friends came, iand many people who did not know him, but knew of his artwork, including some other famous artists like Lauzet and Lucien Pisarro. Behind the closed coffin, all of his last paintings were arranged so that everyone could see his beautiful art. Flowers also surrounded the coffin, which was covered with a simple white sheet.

It is essential to remember that, since Vincent liked yellow flowers so much, yellow flowers could be seen everywhere at the funeral. His friends and family thought the van Gogh would have liked to have been buried with yellow flowers, especially since he thought the color was bright and hopeful.

At the foot of his coffin was also his easel, his painting stool, and all of his paintbrushes. It was a sad funeral, but it also a fitting farewell for one of the best-known and loved painters in the world. Despite the fact that Vincent van Gogh likely committed suicide and died from his injury, the funeral was still a time for remembrance. Everyone there looked at his paintings and marveled at their beauty and their thought. If people did not like Vincent van Gogh's paintings before, they started to now  They began to see the beauty and the humanity in his work—it was something like they had never seen before.

# Chapter 11: The Legacy of the Artist

A student can learn about Vincent van Gogh's life from beginning to end, but that does not mean that he or she necessarily *understands* van Gogh and the implications that his work had on the world. Why exactly was he such a gigantic deal? Why, over one hundred and fifty years later, are we still studying his work? Why does a simple painting of a vase of sunflowers hold such significance to us? What separates van Gogh from the thousands of other artists who have been forgotten by popular history?

There is something about van Gogh's art that resonates within the human mind and soul. There is something special about it.

Vincent van Gogh did not just *paint* things. He poured all of his emotion and his thoughts into his work, and this is why it is so real to us. This is something that is rarely seen today, with so many artists painting just to get money. Van Gogh never started as an artist, and found that it was his true calling later in life. In a single decade, he completed dozens of works that are relished by students, scholars, and historians across the world.

Many artists have tried to recreate van Gogh's paintings, usually to no avail. It seems like van Gogh had a special talent that other people are rarely able to tap into. He certainly had a way with the paintbrush, creating beautiful drawings that combined emotion with excellent style.

Vincent van Gogh gave the world what is now known as the "artist persona." This is what people assume to be the typical personality of artists: moody and unsuccessful, yet willful and committed. He gave plenty of culture to the world of art and the set the stage for dozens of new celebrities to take the world stage and become famous with their artwork.

Van Gogh also gives hope to millions of people that suffer from mental disorders each year. It seems like mental disabilities are a growing problem as we become more aware of their presence in our society. They are here, and we must discover a way to deal with them. Van Gogh showed the world that, even though his mental disorders were sometimes too much for him to handle, he was still able to become a world-renowned poet, famous for more than a hundred years after his death. Depression, seizures, and bipolar disorder were no match for van Gogh; he took them on head-first, and succeeded.

During the final two months of his life, many of his paintings were darker in color than they had been previously. It is clear to see that Vincent van Gogh was not doing too well. He put so much of his energy and his emotion into his painting that viewers are able to know about the artist just by looking at his paintings.

It is important to understand that van Gogh's work was crucial in the development of the *Expressionist* movement. What was expressionism? It was similar to *impressionism* in a way, except that expressionism was focused on getting the artist to show emotion and spirit through their painting. Whether it was an expression of general feelings or an expression of the artist's identity is up to the creator.

During the time, many of the impressionists were too strictly confined within their own loose rules, and many of them were afraid to break the guidelines. They simply wanted to paint realistic paintings, and nothing more. Van Gogh took everything to a whole new level by fueling his paintings with intense emotion, emotions that he would share with his audience. One of the reasons that people continue to look at his art is because of the way they feel when they think about it.

Expressionist artists followed in Vincent van Gogh's steps, admiring his colors and the way in which he portrayed the world around him. His skill with the paintbrush is revered; very few artists have been able to pull off the same effect with the same emotion and feeling behind it.

Many famous artists were influenced by the work of Vincent van Gogh, including Pablo Picasso, Joan Miro, Willem de Kooning, and Francis Bacon. Without van Gogh's initial steps into the world of expressionism and experimentation, many artists would never have been as successful as they were. This especially includes Pablo Picasso, arguably one of the most famous artists to ever live. Picasso was involved in a type of are called *Cubism*—but before he committed to cubism, many of his paintings had elements of van Gogh's style sprinkled throughout them.

One thing is absolutely for sure—the world has been taken in the grips of van Gogh-mania. Throughout the world, people are obsessed with Vincent van Gogh and his artwork, hanging his paintings in houses and office buildings, putting the designs on bags and other souvenir items, and converting restaurants into places that are specifically designed to be van Gogh-themed. It is extremely rare for any other artist to be idolized in this way. So what's so different about van Gogh? Why doesn't da Vinci have his own chain of restaurants?

People seem to connect well with Vincent van Gogh, probably because he went through so many issues, just like many of us do. He understood the poor, and he understood rejection and failure. But despite the many times that he found himself faced with the roughest of troubles, he was always able to pull through and create beautiful works of art. Obviously, in the end, van Gogh was defeated by his debilitating mental illnesses, but he did not go down without a fight.

In one of his letters, Vincent van Gogh wrote "Love is eternal -- the aspect may change, but not the essence. There is the same difference in a person before and after he is in love as there is in an unlighted lamp and one that is burning. The lamp was there and was a good lamp, but now it is shedding light too, and that is its real function. And love makes one calmer about many things, and that way, one is more fit for one's work."

As always, Vincent used light as a symbol for hope. When one looks at his paintings, it is impossible to miss the fact that van Gogh was particularly hopeful. Many of his works are beautiful and bright. To him, this meant that he was searching for a way out of his depression; he only wanted happiness. To us, this means that we can appreciate how he felt because we have felt it at one time ourselves. The art of Vincent van Gogh is the art of the human mind and the human experience.

As long as there are humans in the world, we will be studying Vincent van Gogh, his paintings, and his letters. They tell the story of a frail human who sought happiness and peace from one of the only thing that separates humans from other animals: art. Vincent van Gogh is a tribute to humans everywhere, and his paintings will continue to be celebrated and revered.

# Resources

http://www.biography.com/people/vincent-van-gogh-9515695

http://www.vangoghgallery.com/misc/overview.html

http://www.ibiblio.org/wm/paint/glo/impressionism/

http://www.vangoghgallery.com/influences/post-impressionists.html

http://www.vangoghgallery.com/painting/potatoindex.html

http://designercityline.wordpress.com/2010/03/15/writing-analysis-of-the-potato-eaters-by-van-gogh/

http://www.artble.com/artists/vincent_van_gogh/paintings/starry_night/more_information/analysis

http://www.vggallery.com/visitors/002.htm

http://usatoday30.usatoday.com/travel/destinatio
ns/2009-10-11-van-gogh-letters-
amsterdam_n.htm

http://www.vangoghmuseum.nl/vgm/index.jsp?p
age=425&lang=en&section=sectie_museum

http://www.artyfactory.com/art_appreciation/art_
movements/expressionism.htm

Made in United States
North Haven, CT
23 April 2022

18499475R00055